For Henry D. Thoreau

Acknowledgements

I would like to thank David Nettleingham, Karin Pilipp and Natalia Bondarenko for their valuable suggestions and support during the final editing of this work.

REQUIEM

AUF EINER STELE

twelve fragments

Federico Federici

THE
CONVERSATION
PAPERPRESS

First published 2010 by
THE CONVERSATION PAPERPRESS
Upper Roundell, ME13 8ES, UK
www.conversationpoetry.co.uk

ISBN 978-0-9563137-4-4

Printed and bound in the UK by
the University of Kent Print and Design Centre.

Requiem

auf einer Stele

am Neckar

This poem is a stone, a still voice on the river-bed at the mercy of rushing water. It is the deciphered scratches and black stains on its surface.

This poem is a conversation in the green rooms of the woods where a hollow reed-throat sings beside a death-bed. It is the inexhaustible industry of the trout to compete upriver, and time abruptly halted by the sea. The stone is unmoving.

Långt inne i mörkret. Världen går mot sitt slut.

] thou comest

] thou com[es]t

with perfect precision ·
] · [
] quae tanta fuit tibi causa vivendi?
Neque vita causa fuit!

] scribant de te alii [
[ ]
] iamˌ petraeˌ sumite vires!
] quamve bibistis aquam?[†]
›2‹

] bl[es][se]d ·

] but of space and time ›1.5‹
[ ] ·
Есть только небо[ℵ]
fr. 1.

[†] ...] quale fu il motivo tanto grande della vita?/ Non la vita, certo!// ...] altri scrivano di te [...// [ ]/ ...] e voi, pietre, rianimatevi!/ ...] che acqua mai beveste?/ ...]

[ℵ] there is only sky

]
das ist eine im feld gefundene stele
das ist ein im fluss gefundener stein
dies die im körper gefundenen knochen[iii]

dies materiales fuerunt[iv] ›1.4‹ shortestˌ infrequent
[

] carboniferous tubers awakening
[of] ›1.3‹
] black alluvial fingers
] veins winding along
eye-pebbles and flints [ˌ curving the fields where
there is no endˌ [›2.2‹ did not want to end
to the abandoned land
] · I'm the old riverˌ the whole riverˌ
the understanding of it
] река–это я[v]

fr. 2 A.

] und das sind die polierten knochen
der poeten in meinem fleisch[vi]
[

[iii] this is a stele found in the field/ this is a stone found in the river/ these are the bones found in the body

[iv] [those] were material days

[v] I'm the river

[vi] and these are the polished bones/ of the poets within my flesh

] как лес[vii]

] redeemer of waters [
[bla]ck old tree-line in the flicker of storm ·

fr. 2 B.

carved on the names of the dead and on the short amen of grassˌ when the river freezes ten degrees below zeroˌ and its voice grows old in the parable of thunder · ¦das hart gefrorene licht[viii]¦ a peat-pit under-earˌ where a closer shout could not be heard · the birdsong left mute hearts in a cage of wings · curved images lie beneathˌ awaiting old oak roots to be sucked up from hollows · ¦das wort schwitzt durch das eis[ix]¦ · cormorants hanging over the moor pecked up patches of schist · ›2.1‹ you too lost yellow bonesˌ black paws and twigsˌ dense nerves left on rocksˌ ¦wie raues heuˌ totes gelbes gras[x]¦ sweeping plectrums through the light cry of springˌ when rain was typing on April waterˌ flowing slowly beneath us or close by · ¦mein gesicht geht von mir weg und bleibt fern[xi]¦ · something forever gone in the work of words · ¦vor mir steht ein alter unfruchtbarer apfelbaum · meine

---

[vii] like a wood

[viii] the light frost hardened

[ix] the word oozes from ice

[x] as rough hay, dead yellow grass

[xi] my face goes away from me and keeps far

müden hände zittern[xii]¦ · [*-12-*] lithe ants slowly climb, weighing nothing in the invisible discipline of leaves, of the grass which makes the wind articulate · ¦es ist zeit, die stunden schweben voraus[xiii]¦ · all falls onto the seasons of your face, for all comes as a season, ¦aus dem wald, meinem oeden kopf[xiv]¦ · spring time is yet as perfect for death as the winter threshold, hacked by the axe on the river's edge, where the moon-gap moves forward one millimetre each night · ¦oh wie leise tropft das licht aus jeder ader![xv]¦

fr. 3.

[the] tongue of the dead in the mouth of the living speaks the numbness of exile, a heavy brow of such severe mercy · the tips of fingers gather numberless creases encompassing a new black hole when the day's done · its odd twist and the continual straining makes time move straight on the skin-line and time succeeds time, neat as expected, powdered, ¦von stern zu stein[xvi]¦, a thousand ages per minute, under silent granite, unheard and

---

[xii] before me an older fruitless apple tree stands . my weak hands shiver

[xiii] it is time: the hours hanging overhead

[xiv] out of the woods, from my wasting head

[xv] oh how quietly light drips from every vein!

[xvi] from star to stone

reconciled · I have myself removed the finest minutes, seconds maybe, the last few thousand blinks of your eyelids · may you live or die now, off time · ¦blinde rosen sind ohne dornen[xvii]¦ · [*-5-*] vowels bloom on the stems of dead flowers · bones spelled out upon the grass · ¦du spürst das wortlose wasser in allen deinen knochen[xviii]¦ · ›2.0‹ ear-trap, mouth-well, gravitating, sinking · the whole river's pressure on the weirs of veins ·

fr. 4.

[*-10-*] ground-down words hesitate, bare in the fire, blazing, pulverized, ›1.5‹ [flesh]-compelled and exposing nerves, a stirred-up start to inarticulate occurrences, and against the reticence of silence a chorus of consonants and vowels, each joining another as though speech were the last cry of hope · ¦das wort-innere ist leer · richte nicht das wort L·I·E·B·E an mich[xix]¦ · [*-4.3-*] they came to this side in a twitch of nerves, language tracery in a lapse of the brain's currents, crossing doleful distances, jinking along stretched wires, to pursue the inborn patches and patterns and space and

---

[xvii] not a thorn on a blind rose

[xviii] you experience wordless water in all of your bones

[xix] the inside of a word is empty . don't speak to me the word "love"

time to which all worlds conform in becoming · ¦wär dann nicht alles nur physik? leicht zu verstehenˌ wie man anderswo sagt[xx]¦ · such things get framed in the sensitive mass of the body keeping it uprightˌ the rational sum of age and weight · [

] dust and resting dust · fire and true fire[xxi] [

אֵשׁ = γאֵשׁ$_0$

[ˌ ashesˌ]

] death is synchronized by birth · time's intake · ¦du bist wieder wegˌ weg aus dem raum und weg aus der zeit[xxii]¦ · beyond the absolute centre of Copernicusˌ beyond the absolute of Galileo's restˌ lie the lines of eventsˌ the space-time path shut behindˌ and in the late reward of rememberingˌ whose proper time delays in the general mess of failure and success · we all glide forth as time grows old between two stationsˌ like the light in the pupil when the eyelid is up and its bloodless liquid drips · ¦du warst innen raum und raum war zeit und umgekehrt · es ist ein so großes

---

[xx] wouldn't all be physics then? so easy to understand – it is said elsewhere

[xxi] here I have deliberately used "dust" instead of "mass" and "fire" instead of "time". אֵשׁ [esh] = fire and אֵשׁ$_0$ stands for "true fire"

אֵשׁ = γאֵשׁ$_0$ is a relativistic relationship in the frame of space-time

[xxii] away you are again, away from space and away from time

problem, aber das prinzip wirkt so einfach[xxiii]¦ · some abstraction, needed first in all manner of things · a logic, level with anxiety points us to the right end, to a sort of purest affection between oxymorons and paradoxes · [*-12-*] a visible, delightful, propitious and dignified end, dipped into a lachrymal pond · ›1.3‹ [a] votive burial among grass roots that awaits us at the edge of midwinter woods, or on a feldspar bed among gold burnished thorns, seeking another womb · ¦durch deine raum-zeit läuft ein kleines unvermutetes licht[xxiv]¦ ·

] it's no use being dead with a little help from time · the pe[a]l of bells, slow rattle of bones, both wrapped in a dried-skin packing case hung upon nothing ›2.0‹ н · а · т · ю · р · м · о · р · т[xxv] ·

fr. 5.

ribs vibrate with the sound of twigs gathering tails of air in the vacuum of silence · thick bites on bones leave open spaces · a clock ticks – dig a deep den, clothed, closed in a hiding-place, little ache, black niche · A M E N · what is their song? there's

---

xxiii you were space inside and space was time and vice versa . it is so big a problem, but the principle looks easy

xxiv through your space-time runs a small unexpected light

xxv still life

no end to the faintness of the green above the treesˌ the wrongs of timeˌ the fated and lamented birth and death that never heal · דּ[xxvi] you are your last self · the world of spirit knows its wayˌ ›1.7‹ snow quietly falling in a blind alleyˌ old low track that seems perpetual from behind windows and doors ›1.2‹ until its contractionˌ its water in the late spasm of winter · that is what infinity may be ¦stell dir einen streifen schnee vorˌ in dem kein licht ist und auch sonst nichtsˌ bist du so hell?[xxvii]¦ ›1.5‹

] г[де][xxviii] [когда ладо[нь] бела[xxix] ·

]   ]я[xxx] [ˌ

ˌ   [-*10*-] отпечаток места [xxxi] ·

noisy tunesˌ bony things loosely hanging at a wallˌ this unfinished wail stirring up the parched throats of ghostsˌ fingers drumming on the empty size of a wooden box · desiccation traces the prints on lenses and panes at the heart of glassˌ the vitreous inoperancy of eyes under many layers of frost · ¦aufgeschlagene augen in der dunkelheit der

---

[xxvi] דּ [dèlet] = door

[xxvii] set a strip of snow before you, in which there is no light and nothing else – are you so bright?

[xxviii] where

[xxix] when the palm is white

[xxx] I (?)

[xxxi] imprint of the place

hände[xxxii]¦ · E C C E S I G N U M C R U C I S · ›1.4‹ a word's letters paralysed on the glassˌ the lip's standstill · ¦kein wasser mehrˌ kein wortˌ ein ganzer molekulartraum aus deinem atem ging aus der ferne vorbei[xxxiii]¦ ·

ˌ] in the tragic age above usˌ from its extensive noiseˌ from all its massive wordsˌ missed timbres raise from a solo twist of leaves in the miniature of grassˌ from an intricate twitch of fibres tuned-up under-skin over the coarseness of bonesˌ or from the inarticulate tongue too quick to the word's trick · all that seems accessibleˌ inscribed already – a creak of nailsˌ requiring total careˌ brings little more consciousness to the unpredictable · that is not in itself desirableˌ ›1.2‹ a good fortune or notˌ it owes to those circumstances and the secrecy of gloves · ¦wie zart du bist und wie allein dein körper ist![xxxiv]¦ [ˌ

›1.0‹

ˌ] во[ло]сокˌ[xxxv] what was to be in the turmoil and smoke of a wedding scene? the dust on a grey sleeve from the collarˌ fallenˌ will get no relief on the maddening cord velvet strips · what dead trees leave: a tremor along

---

[xxxii] opened eyes in the darkness of the hands

[xxxiii] no more water, no word, a full molecular dream from your breath has passed from afar

[xxxiv] how frail you are and how alone your body is!

[xxxv] a hair

ascending spiralsˌ uneven stairs to heaven in undisturbed woods · ¦die nacht weitet sich zur hautˌ unendliches dunkel an meinem gesicht[xxxvi]¦ · leaves that fall save the likeness of one part to its whole · and reeds and bush twigs and fernsˌ like short frogs' leaps at the edge of the dark[xxxvii]ˌ are all images and motions of unequal durationˌ bent on the river sheet · direction is to move in measureˌ to match up with incompetent eyes and stare at new white transparencies of day · ¦es ist die zeitˌ die zählt[xxxviii]¦ · ›1.9‹

] can you see nothing?

[*-14.5-*]ˌ ответ[xxxix] ·

fr. 6.

at eight sharp rooms are dead aroundˌ await another seasonˌ another word of rest · no direction echoes in the sound of footsteps · mother eyes within other eyes look after things windward far hence[xl] · is there an empty guitar there amid air-nodesˌ or a wrung neck hanging from the oak fingersˌ or a mid-air nestˌ or the swans' cage? ›1.2‹ what falls apart in there? circles of gnats · antsˌ

[xxxvi] night widens to skin, unending darkness on my face

[xxxvii] *balzi di rane ai margini dell'ombra*

[xxxviii] it's time that counts upward

[xxxix] answer

[xl] *gli occhi di madre negli occhi governano le cose*

lining up climb a dead fish head now thoughtlessˌ do the sort of the material work which is closest to the livingˌ and by means of the force that makes the worldˌ for through the body only life is delayed · ¦wächst auch auf den toten seen der augen gras?[xli]¦

fr. 7.

мир – камни и снег[xlii] · things cast shadowsˌ perpendicular to the nowhere of papers upon which homes are builtˌ found cities on the ruins of namesˌ damp with sticky inks · words de-text themselvesˌ collideˌ ride to the gap of a breathˌ prostrate under the line of the last tongue · ¦so spricht das gedicht wort für wort · der zweifel sitzt im wort[xliii]¦ · speaking at silent turns[xliv] the speech becomes invisibleˌ a wisp of air scattering consonants and vowelsˌ soundless quantaˌ shortest figures of matterˌ[xlv] in which this world waves · all is restless subtractionˌ open circles and holes from the breathˌ heat out of the dark measure of throats · ¦und aus den augen äußert sich die welt · das licht wächst[xlvi]¦ · massless light travels alone inscribed

---

[xli] does grass grow also on the dead seas of eyes?

[xlii] the world: stones and snow

[xliii] so the poem speaks word by word . doubt resides in words

[xliv] *parlando accanto a svolte silenziose*

[xlv] *le cifre della materia*

[xlvi] and out of eyes, the world pronounces itself . light grows

with millions of unthinkable years, flitting away through the amnesia of distant space on a tape of stars, on the sleep of an empty field, with its load of buried petals, swallowed either side in the stones and the grassy smell of trees on the unheard marching of ants – across the withering annunciation of winds and all shabby equipment – as sailors cut the biting fish's guts with no gaze of ecstasy · ¦so frisst sich die zeit in den raum[xlvii]¦ · ›1.4‹ bright windows past and future, we sit before them, behind wet, flimsy curtains, awaiting the end of day to take notes in a journal under lamplight by the sole strength of devotion, hoarding new words from old despair ¦wenn dir das tageslicht egal ist[xlviii]¦ · burning · burn[ing] · pushing lives above light, above whiteness · a topmost branch sprays pollen and leaves from the centre of darkness · it cannot be deciphered though, paralysed on windows or in a mirror forged which both eyes held still · dripdripdrip-drip upon short irregular patterns beginning at the top corner · the whole enclosed work of waters quietly consumes old stones and walls, coated in a thin film of moss · 100,000 million placeless pebbles fall in 100,000 million little circles of light in the riverbed · all obeys the dying verse

---

[xlvii] this is the way time consumes itself in space

[xlviii] if daylight makes no difference to you

reverberating out of chaosˌ singing in sandy gardensˌ hunting stony words ›1.7‹ · glowing · glowing · glowing · where the dead men left warm stonesˌ the water sleep flows in the very integer of shape and bone · название реки в море исчезает[xlix] ·
молчание ·
молчание[l] · ˌ
] ¦das radio schweigt und gott auch · das unsichtbare ohr auf der uhr[li]¦ ·
[*-12.1-*] одиночество ˌ ·
одиночество[lii] ·
fr. 8.

no mirth at human follyˌ but an old owl lament · water and fire encounter no defenceˌ nor clean sheltersˌ nor roots · all preys departed · on spring nights following the fish path down streamˌ with an ear to the line of airˌ sidewaysˌ but there's no fish inˌ no path to fish inˌ none foreseen down-stream · spring nights among the rocksˌ fishingˌ at the turn of tideˌ waiting for the dark to fill the netˌ the burial of the unmanoeuvrable moon set white

---

[xlix] the name of the river disappears into the sea
[l] silence . silence
[li] the radio keeps silent and god too . the invisible ear on the hour
[lii] loneliness . loneliness

bones in the cobwebbed creel · forgetful dust, brown banks of rubbish, waste crags, twigs casting shadows on a greenish mud · I wept, like under the burden of a bag of snow · I wept · so only the dead can contest for those who have never been · I wept · the dead, the spirits, ¦die schlangenfische nach der engelsstunde · der schmerz lässt nach[liii]¦ · hear the faint voice of the bones the eye sees, those sectioned by the endless wind playing upon sleep in the calm hope of prayer, like briar on fire[liv], which the quiet voice of age has not yet reached, nor can you retract · consult the map of fingers in the gaps between bones tied up like grass, have your wishbone part and hope · bodies never finished · days sprout at the edge of days · ¦lasst die zahlen in ruhe · keine theorie · keine vision vor dir[lv]¦ · all counts number to infinity, point to an end which cannot bear reality, though, for there's no real end · the end itself is endless · numbers rim the multiplicity of the world ¦und nur das rechnen im schlaf · die null schmerzt in der letzten nacht des alten jahres[lvi]¦ ·

] не так[lvii], ›1.1‹

[liii] the fishing snake after the angel hour . sorrow lessens

[liv] *come infocato rovo*

[lv] leave numbers quiet . no theory . no vision before you

[lvi] and only the calculations in sleep . zero only does harm on the last night of the old year

[lvii] not like this

] не то[lviii] [

[*-7.2-*] ˌ · время идёт[lix]

] ¦п·о·п·о·з·в·о·н·о·ч·н·и·к·у·р·е·к·и¦[lx] ˌ

fr. 9.

the namedˌ the unnamedˌ the many articulations deepenˌ empty mental wires through little piles of cells · the ancient bone-chip never stops singing its perpetual angelusˌ inarticulate and delicate · the body left with many soundless voicesˌ utterance of infolded silence ›1.3‹ · the named withers into the unnamed beyond the world of figures on a dry sheet of nerves[lxi]ˌ like short rain showers warped in glass · my lifeˌ my deathˌ in both eyes and hands upon both awaited fatesˌ open wide[lxii] · nor can one touch something unnamed ¦und nicht ein leeres zeichen[lxiii]¦ ›0.3‹ intractable in the mind · [*-1.1-*] nothing but the trying between dark and darkˌ April and Aprilˌ disconnecting time with the late bloom of thyme in the garden's ashes and the harvests rhythm on behalf of seasons · ›2.0‹ precisely nothing · days fall apart like the water

---

[lviii] not this

[lix] time passes by

[lx] по позвоночнику реки: along the river spine

[lxi] *in un'asciutta pagina, foglio di nervi*

[lxii] *la mia vita, la mia morte accadono negli occhi come nelle mani, sui due destini attesi, spalancate*

[lxiii] and not an empty sign

insects gravitating in a disturbance of earthly lightˌ light-addled in the new sleepˌ or snow iced on the pole tips · мир врастает в камень · земная тишина в асфальтовой луже[lxiv] ›2.1‹ ˌ

ˌ] головокружение[lxv]ˌ ˌ · [
-11.1-]

fr. 10.

›1.3‹¦es schneit! es schneit! es schneit! es ist spätˌ denn was heiβt schon zeitheit? licht der wirklichkeit?[lxvi]¦ · arms curving over empty holes define us · precisely nothing that nothing holds · he who was lost has not been called back yet from his warm haze of spring · how easily the inaudible grace of solitude fills the same place! · snow continues to fallˌ vowels and snowˌ atonal snow piling up on both hands in the tall grassˌ holding the world-weight downward · we never touch thingsˌ things attract us · not much else · were voices there along this black amount of waterˌ someone would hear us firstˌ muttering like a newˌ clean spring spilt among dry boulders · let us stand still with the river like the waters do · the sleepy

---

[lxiv] the world grows in the stone . terrestrial silence in the asphalt puddle

[lxv] vertigo

[lxvi] it is snowing! snowing! snowing! it is late, so what does *zeitheit* mean? [temporality] . the light of reality?

rhyme of the dead hour calls · the word half spelt͵ the word half written for fear of too much abstraction lie under the water's haste · the real names͵ the good ones thronged into leggy shrubs glint in their finitude · nothing else but names͵ ideograms on thin leaves͵ names͵ nerves͵ stems whose fine ends are not flowers but stars · it's what we live in͵ asleep · that which was a house is dust now · ב [lxvii] · a hollow stone · the inside of the house is between the trees · wood after fire keeps a tepid hope · frozen roots fed on ashes underfoot jut out · ¦hier also hältst du dich versteckt? die klarheit͵ die sternenkunst machen dir so viel angst[lxviii]¦ · lonesome lilacs bleed among the wreckage · ›1.1‹ ͵ [sw]amp fern͵ no reflection in the canal dredged by the fire-black oil lamp · the sacrifice remains͵ foundation to a new beginning͵ redeems us with old hints of ardour and birth ·

[¦zwei tränen[lxix] [*-6.1-*] ¦das schwere[lxx]¦͵
›3.1‹
͵¦die beiden türen der welt[lxxi]¦]

[· *-8.1-*] ·

[lxvii] ב [bayit] = house

[lxviii] have you hidden here then? the clarity, the art of stars make you fear so much

[lxix] two tears

[lxx] the weight

[lxxi] the two doors of the world

снежные слоги – без упования[lxxii] · [·

· ›0.3‹

]¦und du dich flüstern hörst [lxxiii]¦

] *ach* matter oscillates in silence · ¦auf dem schädeldach, ein hohler stein, ein kortikaler irrgang[lxxiv]¦ · cubes within cubes carry voices through with no complaint,[lxxv] tiny spasms in the purest emptiness of volumes · a closed network of wrinkles and cells writhe under some abstraction of time · last equation solved, pre-day shine · ¦auge und mund sind leer · welche außenwelt erkennt sich selbst?[lxxvi]¦ no regular intersection of words, no vibrating beats of lips, no effect of mostly regular breathing, no need to do · nor can physics impinge on beauty from the smooth edge of things · ›2.1‹ ¦feine risse auf dem a·u·g·e·n·[h·i·n·t]·e·r·b·i·l·d[lxxvii]¦ ·

fr. 11.

¦metaphysisches gespinst[lxxviii]¦ stones blossom in the friction of water at early spring, under the quiet

---

[lxxii] snow syllables are hopeless

[lxxiii] and you hear yourself whisper

[lxxiv] on the top of the skull, an empty stone, a cortical labyrinth

[lxxv] *trasporta voci senza lamento*

[lxxvi] mouth and eye are empty . what sort of outer world knows itself?

[lxxvii] fine fractures on the [back]-image of the eye

[lxxviii] metaphysical texture

burden of time, carry off the sleep of thousands of years, away in the due course of the river · greened detritus and grit fall nowhere but in the sedge grass under the black gum · the world's substance divines us and seeps through vacant lots of dark, what it comes from, where it goes · ¦finsternis[lxxix]¦ F · I · N · I · S · T · E · R · R · A · E[lxxx] · dust fluctuates a while carelessly through the thick barrier of light, in the late hush of day, in a brighter sphere, evading nothing · ›3.0‹ its aim is too high a purpose · the portrait of a dumb clock-face shines in shafts of sunlight · ¦in einem hellen augenblick[lxxxi]¦ its fingers count round figures only, while others go through iron teeth and gears inside ¦um aus 1 allein die zeit zu machen[lxxxii]¦ · [*-10-*] time sprouts unmoving from whole trees folding, calm stems defused bending under flower migraines · ›0.6‹ hollow stars go hunting eternity, extinguishing thirst and black holes in a short pulse of light · what was burning ended in light, the burial of nothing, the last link of remembering · the late bliss of wise, stiff, oblivious tongues · small creatures promiscuously dying in their quiet, quick transcendence · and not to start again · and not to

---

[lxxix] darkness

[lxxx] at the land end-line

[lxxxi] in a bright instant

[lxxxii] to make Time out of 1 alone

come to an end · even while the dust ends · the cause and end of all · the still end when it ends ·

[· · › 1.4 ‹

] где мы были?[lxxxiii]

fr. 12.

[lxxxiii] where have we been?

Rules and tips about symbols

Words and signs between open-closed square brackets have been either recovered (when hardly decipherable) or restored according to the closest reliable meaning (when completely missing).

Blank space means that a whole single line is missing.

Open square brackets on different lines span the whole surface of some missing and unrecoverable text.

Numbers between open-closed square brackets indicate the length (inches) of a fracture-erased set of words (unrecoverable).

Isolated closed square brackets indicate that we can gauge that a consistent part of the text has been lost from that point backwards, but that we can't exactly delimit it.

Isolated open square brackets indicate that we can gauge that a consistent part of the text has been lost from that point on but we can't exactly delimit it.

Words between two vertical broken bars indicate those more deeply carved in the stone.

Numbers between right or left-pointing angled quotation marks indicate the depth (inches) of a hole in the stone (deeper than 1 inch).

Lower short vertical strokes indicate evident scratches on the surface of the stone.

Interpuncts indicate moss spots and other stains.

Federico Federici was born in Liguria in 1974. He is a researcher and teacher of physics, a translator (from German, Russian and English) and a writer. He has published a number of books of prose and poetry under the name Antonio Diavoli as well as texts and critical papers in reviews, anthologies and internet journals. He translated and saw through the first book in Italian by the Hindi poet Rati Saxena, and the posthumous work of Russian poet Nika Turbina. He is editor of *л*: the Italian edition of *Conversation* magazine, within the Conversation International Poetry Project.

He has taken part in festivals and readings in Italy, Germany and Poland, picture exhibitions in Italy and Germany, and video poetry and short-film festivals in Italy, Germany and Venezuela. In 2009 he was awarded the Lorenzo Montano Prize for his poetry collection *L'opera racchiusa* - the first book of poems to be published in his own name.

http://leserpent.wordpress.com/